The Family Business:
From the Carriage to the Court!

Tracy Leonard Jamison

Editor:
Audrey Lancho

Graphic Design:
Olivia Pro Designs

INTRODUCTION

I'm new to this game; I'm not quite an animal. There are rules to this book; I wrote you a manual!

A step-by-step booklet for you not to FORGET!

The 10 Book Commandments:
A Guide to Read and Enjoy this Book

1. Be Prepared and Open Minded

2. Let Your Guard Down, You Don't Know Everything!

3. The Grind is Not for The Feint of Heart!

4. Business is Never Personal!

5. Honesty is the Best Policy!

6. Integrity and Loyalty go Hand in Hand!

7. Some Names Have Been Changed to Protect the Guilty!

8. Less is MORE!

9. This is a Guide, not a Gospel!

10. This is OUR STORY!

DEDICATION

This book is dedicated to my father, Leonard Joseph Jamison - SIP King - the man who was the original CEO of The Family Business. Pop was the first one to put a ball in my hands, he was my first coach, and he was my first and only agent. The book is also dedicated to the underdog with the heart of a lion, who was never given the chance to be great. I have also sprinkled hoop knowledge through personal reflections in this text, with the hopes of helping you gain perspective on how to win when so many obstacles are put in place for you to lose.

With hoops, our journey has taught me that you meet great people, sketchy people, and people who are super clueless. At the end of the day, regardless of what sport you have your child in, loyalty to your child is the only thing that matters. And the quicker you realize what the end goal is, the easier the ride will be. You as a parent need to try and not live vicariously through your child's dreams, but instead allow them fall in love with the sport organically, with no hidden agendas and no pressure if they do not reach your expectations for success.

And last but not least, this is dedicated to my Kings (sons) and my Wisdom (wife) for bearing with me all of these years, trusting my madness, and trying to figure it out on the fly. "It" being travel hoops (AAU), city summer circuit, and just balancing hoops with the importance of schoolwork and being a great citizen. It was never easy, and the plan was never really structured or mapped out with the end goal in focus.

Ma Dukes, Pop (SIP King), Norma, Juju, Trey, Lauren, Jaden, Sharon, Traci Lauren, and Ma (Emma). We did it! Love y'all immensely and there is no me without you!

Thanks also to Uncle Bubb for helping me develop my ball handling skills on those hot summer days, you truly were there when I needed that South Side (We Outside) grit!

POWER Foreword:

On a Saturday evening, there was nothing like receiving messages, filled with stats and videos of how the boys did during their travel tournaments. I could not help but think of how much those point guard skills were passed from their father to the two young men who were now playing at such a high level!

I have known the author since he arrived on this earth. His father, Lennie, was like a mentor to me. With my love for basketball, as I have experienced it as a coach, I became a mentor to him for a season of his life. One day, he came to visit our home in Queens, New York. We went to the park and I was amazed at how much he had developed from the last time I was able to work with him. After that, he took off to become a great basketball player. Before cell phones, I would watch his highlight reels on a VHS tape, and I was so proud of him. Reading this book reminded me so much of the challenges he faced with basketball. Tracy came up in an era when point guards were small, and quick - the captain on the court. When he played ball, his game was reminiscent of "the Little General" (Sherman Douglas) from Syracuse University. As an extension of the coach, the point guard was the coach on the floor, and made sure the game plan was executed at the highest level on both sides of the ball. He was a true point guard - the way he ran the team, and balanced the floor is the same way he balances his family - a natural leader. There is no surprise that he and his wife met on the basketball court during college and ended up raising a basketball family. The game truly runs deep in their DNA. While the love of the game and the talent would no doubt come naturally to the young men, Tracy knew from his own experience as a youth basketball star that he needed to be there to advocate for his boys at each and every opportunity. In the quest to reach the highest level of basketball, the parents who have the money, the time, the support, and the coach's ear, are the ones whose children are most likely to be spotlighted. Work ethic, passion, and skill is not all it takes to become an elite baller. It takes persistence, overcoming the roadblocks and exposure. Other parents will have no problem stealing the spotlight from your child in order for their child to shine brighter. It is difficult to keep the love of the game in your heart when you realize that it is polluted. As a former basketball parent myself, I can concur with the sentiments of the author…don't just drop your kids off.

As one of the true New York City Point Gods, Mark Jackson, said, **"You cannot disrespect the caterpillar and rave about the butterfly"**. I enjoyed the reading. Lace up your kicks and enjoy the run. This is WAY more than just basketball…

Winford Bethea
The Big Unc
Inwood Street, Southside Jamaica, New York
#InwoodStrong

THE GAME PLAN

GENESIS (THE FOUNDATION, WOMB TO THE HARDWOOD)

THE FEVER (EAGERNESS TO BE GOOD)

TURNING THE CORNER

TRAINING METHODS (ON AND OFF THE COURT)

WHAT ARE WE DOING THIS FOR (LOVE OF THE GAME): FATHERS AND THEIR SONS

JEALOUSY AND ENVY

TREY JULIAN AKA 2.0

AAU VS. NOT AAU

RECLASSIFICATION

MY NAME IS MY NAME

LOYALTY AND LOVE, THE UNDERDOG

THE ESSENCE: *BORN READY*

November 11, 1999, started off like any other day with me getting ready for work. My lady was off due to it being Veteran's Day, and with her being a teacher, there wasn't any school. She figured she would take me to work and then go see her mother in New York. Since she wasn't due to give birth until Thanksgiving, she was not prepared for what our first had in store for her!
She had been feeling uneasy, thinking it was because we had Mickie Dee's late the night before. Once she got Uptown, her discomfort became too much to bear, and she called her doctor. She was told it was not the food from the night before, but instead, that Baby Jamison was ready to make his debut!

Traveling back to Jersey with her nephew, niece, and Moms in tow, my lady headed to the doctor's office in Bayonne, getting pulled over by the police in the process. The officer didn't give her a ticket; there was no hiding the fact that this was really an emergency!

I was at work, so I had to get a ride from a friend and meet the family at the hospital, with crazy thoughts traveling in my mind: am I ready? Is she? Are we? IS ANYONE?
Side note, is anyone ever really ready for parenthood?
I digress. . .To say the least, I was a basket case, but I had to be strong, not show any emotions (which was difficult at the time. Next book) and be there because it was really that time to step up and handle what had been bestowed upon me, us, etc.! # Let's Go!

So, by then, we had a waiting room full of TiTi's (Aunties), Grands, Cousins, etc. and the moment had come with much stress, restraint (next, next book), crying, smiles, etc., and the introduction of the one that the world would simply know as JuJu. He arrived crying, but once he heard my voice and I held him, he began to calm. Yes, we had a bouncing baby boy, and the show was ready to begin!

From the onset, it seemed that Juju was destined to play ball. I say that for the simple fact that he seemed to have a ball with him in the womb, meaning it would be a miracle to ever see him without one. By the time he was three or four, living in the Bronx section of New York, he would walk around the neighborhood bouncing a ball. If he came to visit me at work, in the sneaker store, he would be dribbling around the store like he was in a game. The day that I realized what we had on our hands was when we were at a street fair.

In New York, this is an event where they block streets off and have various vendors selling their wares and food. So, that summer afternoon, we were strolling around, vendor to vendor and to keep himself occupied, Ju had his ever-present rock-what we called his ball. Now he was doing his usual, dribbling around, not many tricks, but the usual dribbling, utilizing both hands. As a family we were used to this, and it had become second nature (that's just what he did). But to an outsider, you might've been like, *Wait, shorty little as hell, and he's handling the rock like that*? Yes, he had the ball on a string early. So, by then, we noticed people smiling and giving compliments as we continued to walk.

It was getting late and the fair was almost finished when a couple approached us. This couple was giving Ju his props (dap, big ups, etc.) and asked how old he was. And when we told them he was about five, they asked his name, and if they could take a picture, because they just knew he was going to make it big in the game of basketball.

GENESIS: *THE FOUNDATION, WOMB TO THE HARDWOOD*

The day had been in the making since he was born. Young Ju was ready (or maybe I was) to see what the kid had. My partner in Newark coached Biddies, which were kids under eight, and I wanted to see where we were in the development stage. Ju was now about six, getting ready to turn seven, and as a proud father, I thought my li'l man was ready for the world. Just seeing him handle the ball and his eagerness to be on a court, told me it was indeed time.
So, what did I do? I took him and put him in my guy's hands—meaning I took him to be coached. Whew, he is sooooo small compared to the other kids. Mind you, he was two or three years younger. As a side note, two of these kids turned out to be nationally known!

But no, this was my boy, and deep inside, I knew this was his destiny, and we won't be denied! Okay, so the warmups, the layup lines, started and at first, he seemed comfy, but all that subsided. I was crushed, my boy was shook and intimidated by the other kids. The game had not even started, and they were still warming up. He didn't want to continue, and I didn't want to force him, although with me being selfish, I knew this would be his calling. So, I didn't get upset (at least I didn't show it externally), but instead I comforted him, and we watched the game, all while I was talking to him with the hopes of enticing him into giving it another try. No dice, he was not having any of it. Weekend after weekend, I asked if he wanted to go back, and he was definitely not trying to hear it, and wanted no part of playing in that setting. I even took him to another game, with the hopes of him saying, "Dad can I play?" Sike; it never happened.

We left and in the following days, he was still with the same routine, playing and dribbling his ball wherever we went. There was a park across the street from our house, and Ju had begun to play ball on the monkey bars with his cousins, like it's a basketball court. And with that, it seemed that Ju had found the confidence needed and the journey began.

My wife found a program downtown for kids Ju's age. It was a developmental type of program and me being me, I thought, 'My son don't need that'. And it was pricey, but what the hell, we gave it a try. We went on a Sunday and to say the least, this would be the best investment that we had ever made, and this would open my eyes to what needed to be done to be good early. The session itself wasn't that good, mind you, the director even told me he wasn't sure if this would be good for Ju. Reason being, Ju struggled immensely. He was used to dribbling a man's size ball—who knew there were different sizes? And the kids used youth size. The director said we could give it another try the following week. And me being me, I thought, what do I do?

My answer came quickly: *Go right next door to Modell's and buy a youth basketball and hit the park.* "Who the hell is this dude to tell me he doesn't think this program is for my son? I'm gonna show him!"

On the way uptown, my mind was racing, and I was taking it personally. My son was the next one in a long line of point gods—not point *guards*. 'Gods,' because in New York that was what PGs were. Mind you, Ju was only about six years old, and I had anointed him as the next one.

We headed to Riverdale, a section in the Bronx, and began doing PG drills. Me being a PG, and a pretty good one in my day, I knew what was needed: starting with dribbling drills, and then to the big stuff. Any great PG needs to learn the art of the bounce pass and when to pass on the fast break, which is stopping at the foul line.

THE FEVER: *Eagerness to Be Good*

Okay, I was determined, but not overly, to have my boy play ball. Wifey wanted him to take Communion classes and they were every Saturday morning. This was a conflict with my plans of trying to take Young Ju back to Jersey and play. Monkey Wrench anyone? So, what did I do? I found out that the legendary Gauchos, traveling AAU (Amateur Athletes Union) had a developmental and instructional workout on Saturday/Sunday mornings. #Let'sGo!
I started taking Juju on Sundays, and all was good in the world. He was making his way and it was a good look. We didn't know anyone, which was always good—no handouts and Ju could earn everything that came to him. With this program, they were teaching the kids the basics, dribbling with one hand and head up, shooting, defense, etc. At the end of each four-hour session, they placed the kids on teams and saw what they had learned for the day. Each week, I could see the young God getting more comfortable, and he was starting to bubble. I was not the only one who noticed, other parents started becoming friendly (although their hidden agendas would be revealed later.) and wanting to know who we were. Now came the last session, and they were having an All-Star game. Ju went in and did his thang thang, his team lost but he put on a show. Funny enough, watching him play was a show to me; so entertaining. He won the Sportsmanship award, which was MVP of the losing team. Now he was on shine, and people were really intrigued. Mind you, he was only seven, and most of the kids were eight.

Now we had made a couple of friends, but only some were real ones, and one was a high school coach, who happened to coach older kids in the program. He was putting together an eight and under team. He approached me about Ju and wanted him for the team. He was talking about all of the tournaments that the kids will do, leading up to Nationals. Okay, what was Nationals? This was a National Tournament, where teams from around the country met and played during the summer months for about a week in a southern location. With this, each age group had a different locale, and with eight and under, the destination was Memphis, Tennessee.

Before we got on that flight down south, we took a couple of trips to Baltimore, Maryland. These tournaments were meant as tune-ups to the big show, but they were more of a preview to what we were in store for in Nationals. The team never played together and never seemed to mesh. We seemed to take beatings on the regular, and what should have been learning lessons, never seemed to come across as such. Whether it was parents who didn't have a clue, or kids who just wanted to be kids and didn't care if they won or lost. From day one, the goal with young Ju was to always play hard and leave everything on the floor. And now we were practicing and getting ready for Memphis.

Just me and Ju were destined for the trip. Wifey wasn't too thrilled about visiting Memphis, and it was also going to be my youngest son Trey's birthday on July 4th, Trey, a.k.a. 2.0, was also called I Got Next. We'd be on our way back from Memphis on the fourth, confirming my wife's decision to not go. This would be an experience to fly down with this group of kids and parents, but it would be the last to fly with a big group. So, there was a lot of preparation for a trip of this magnitude. Shopping for kicks, clothes, necessities, etc. Also, purchasing the flights was an experience, and the coach only took cash. *Hmm.* I collected donations from work and had enough to pay for our flights, so I just had to pay for the hotel room, but that wasn't so bad because my Pops—may he rest in peace—was going to meet us down there.

So, we arrived in Memphis with not much to expect, just taking it all in, and attended opening ceremonies. This was where all of the teams gathered to introduce themselves and get a good look at the competition. There, you could see some familiar faces, either from your region or from your travels to others. Once this was over, kids had to sit through a seminar with the Chairman of AAU and they usually gave out some sort of gifts that were school-related, like notebooks, agendas, or pencils. And the topics were usually the same every year, staying in school, maximizing effort and abilities, and staying out of trouble.

Being on the road, long way from home, you usually want your kid to have fun like the other kids. Mind you, Juju was seven and this wasn't a vacation, it was a business trip. The thing was, some kids were in and out of the pool, running around the hotel all hours of the night and when game time (when the lights come on) arrived, these kids were not prepared for the assignment. I'm not really sure why I'm so strict in this sense, but I knew we needed to stay focused on being focused. Needless to say, we proceeded to get punched every game, to say the least.

The highlight of the trip was going to the University of Memphis, meeting Coach Cal, freshman Derrick Rose, and getting time to meet one of my #PointGod idols, Rod Strickland.

TURNING THE CORNER: *Hard Work Paying Off*

Coming off of a year of just playing and practicing without any real plan left a lot to be desired. I met a father from Brooklyn whose son went with our team to Nationals, who had older sons and had been in this grind before. We hit it off immediately and he took us under his wing. I was really green to the whole outdoor circuit; my guy was a blessing—loyalty before royalty.

You name a tournament, we were there. St. John's Rec., Brower Park, Melo & Marbury (free shoes), to name a few. With each event, Juju's name began ringing and we were out in Medina (Brooklyn) so much, they swore we were from that borough.

With playing in the hood and still working out uptown, we start preparing for another run at Nationals. This year it was a whole new team, and since Ju was sort of a veteran, this was his chance to lead the team. The makeup of the team was kind of off, because these set of parents were new to the organization and were looking for carte blanche by buddying up to the coaches. Not really beat for all of the politricks, and maybe that was why we never felt at home with this program—more on that later.
With that being said, with this new crew, it always felt like an us vs them situation. We started hooping in preparation for our second trip to Memphis (and no, wifey was not trekking, because Memphis is not on the destination bucket list). We were making all the usual stops, Island Garden, MIT, etc., and now was the time to get on the plane for our business trip. This year Mom Dukes came with us to help out with the room and enjoy a week full of hoops—being a gym rat is in our DNA.

Having a year under his belt, Ju knew what to expect: no pool, no running around like he has never been outside, but instead, focus on being focused. We struggled the whole weekend and Ju being Ju, he was really hard on himself. Despite being the smallest on the court, 90% of the time, he, just like his younger brother Trey, always wore his heart on his sleeve and left everything on the floor. I never really understood what the other parents had against us, but they always had something to say about Ju. Maybe it was because he was the veteran and was able to do more than their kids; I don't know and truly never cared. After one game, another loss, Ju was frustrated and emotional. We were standing in the lobby and our coach said to
me and Mom Dukes, "He is spoiled!" Well, that didn't go over too well, and from then on, we started to look at him with the side eye.

An assistant coach from Memphis comes up to Ju, and said, "Don't change a thing. Crying means you care, and Derrick Rose cried all the damn time, and look at him now." The assistant coach said to keep working hard, and that Ju was going to be special.

TRAINING METHODS: *On and Off the Court*

"Do this. Do that." This is what you will always hear. If you've played the game or have a natural feel for the game, you can tell what your child needs. It is not about what the new hot method is or what seems to be cool, it's more about knowing your child and his or her deficiencies. The basics to work on, shooting and dribbling, are a given, but mastering is clutch. You should try and steer clear of creating a 'cone kid', a robot-like player. This is a player who only looks good in drills playing with cones or doing orchestrated drills. If you can't have live competition to engage, then you as a trainer should be ready to sweat and help in the drills. This anti-cone work enables the player to act and react to what may actually happen in a live game. Along with all that, comes physical training. For some, you can combine the two, as I seem to have done very often. You can start with throwing or rolling a ball down the court. The player has to sprint down the court, retrieve the ball, grab it and dribble steadily with his head up, back up the court and finish with a jumper or a layup. This method helps with stamina and ball control in the same drill. Rep, reps, and more reps!

They key is to push as hard as possible, but also know your child's limits. I learned the hard way, that there is a big difference between Coach and Dad. I would push, push, and push some more to the point that the young God would tear up. This caused him to stop the workout and proceed to leave the park. The main issue with not knowing your child's limits, is that the kid can burn out and lose interest. Also, positive reinforcement is something that needs to be a focus during training. You can't push, push, and push some more without letting the child know when he or she does something right, or relatively close to being right. You don't want a "game" to hinder you and your child's relationship—it's not that serious!

The most important things that I found out were about ball handling and shooting. Me being a guard in my day, I knew that handling the rock is THE most important thing to work on. I would say, no matter the position, you need to know how to dribble, and especially with the offhand. Start with basics of dribbling without looking down at the ball, going baseline to baseline at full speed, down with dominant hand and back with the weak or offhand. After a couple of reps, you can switch to maybe three dribbles then switch, and three dribbles and switch etc. Next, you can go through the legs and behind the back, and so on. After that, you can proceed to shooting drills.

Form shooting is usually the first drill to tackle. This entails the body being squared to the basket and shooting maybe five to ten feet from the basket and releasing the ball at its highest peak. Reps are the most important aspect of becoming a great shooter. Next, you can venture into the corner, then maybe the extension of the foul line, then top of the key and make your way around the court and get as many reps as possible. The most important aspects of shooting are form, follow-through, and muscle memory, adding up to great mechanics.

Along with dribbling and shooting, strength and conditioning are also important aspects of becoming a serviceable hooper. Running, running, and more running is always a great way to get in shape. Either sprints or long-distance running (road work) are beneficial to getting your wind up. This can help you in the fourth quarter when your opponent is dying and ready to tap out.

WHAT ARE WE DOING THIS FOR?:
Love of the Game – Fathers and Their Sons

The motto 'happiness is free' becomes a way of life when entrenched in this game. I say that to say, when you are involved in a game that is supposed to be so pure and innocent, it is easy to get caught up in the seedy side of things. With that said, you always have a clear game plan and end-game in mind. Most parents, I found, did not play the sport we love. With this, the problems start to arise, focus is lost, and passion is never manifested. Here's an example: the father or mother is so bent on getting full boat (a full scholarship), that they will do any and everything to keep the focus on their child. By no means am I saying that your child should not be your focus, but he or she is just that, *your* focus. People tend to lose focus on others and sabotage the team and, at times, the program for their own personal goals or agendas. When you have not played the sport at a high level, you really can't know what is needed to be great. Everyone has potential, but a parent acting as an agent can kill any potential. Losing focus on the big picture early can be a situation where you can never regain the focus again. As I said before, the question that really needs to be addressed early, is why are we doing this? NBA dreams, free school or just plain fun? Reality will sink in quickly and real life is unforgiving, so if there is no clear path or focus, there will be a lot of confusion along the way. A lot of parents, mostly fathers have that 'mine over yours' mentality and it really poisons the team spirit. The team could be winning, but the hidden agendas are always present. This is crazy because this underlying drama is usually caused by programs looking for the new hot kid, instead of keeping the core team together and building something special. Parents of these kids usually go from program to program, usually killing the team spirit everywhere they go. Bad thing is a lot of these parents never played sports and are living their dreams through their kids' lives. There isn't a dream school, just a dream bag—the league is the main goal.

JEALOUSY AND ENVY

Ever since day one, Ju had the deck stacked against him. Playing with the "Program", he seemed to always be on the outside looking in. No matter how long he played for the program, Ju never seemed to be welcomed with open arms. Always playing hard, always showing respect and loyalty, it just never seemed to be reciprocated. Not so much from the coaches, because you never really know what people are thinking about your product (yes product, because this is a business and your game is for sale….#church), but from the establishment. New flavors of the month (new players) coming to the "Program", seemed to always get first choice on anything, the establishment's ear, and overall preferential treatment over veterans like Ju. Parents were always crying broke and wanting a free ride instead of paying dues, as Ju and other veteran families had done.

Now since Ju was a vet and paid his dues, he pretty much started on the teams that he played for. New people to the teams seemed to have issues with this. Not ever approaching me, but there was always something being said or insinuated to Ju because of favoritism. Oh, it could not be that the youngin' was good and could run a team effortlessly. Nah, it had to be favors being given out. The funny thing is the same people "smiling in ya face" turn out to be backstabbers.

I was brought up with values, and if I did not have anything good to say, I did not say anything. These folks will say everything negative about you and yours to make themselves look good. I mean, I remember this one tournament when our coach was not there, and two parents had to coach. Now I never take things personally, but when my son plays the same position as the coach's son, I know there will be an issue. Don't you know young Ju did not get off the bench the whole game. All good, we are built for the long haul, and it's business! Ju took it in stride, just the way he has been taught. He did not get emotional, but every time he looked my way, it just tore me up inside. Just little things like that teach you that everyone does not have your best interest at heart. Definitely crabs in a barrel mentality. And with me being soft-spoken and not too emotional, people seem to take my kindness for weakness.

My advice to people, and especially fathers, is let everything happen that is going to happen. If it is meant to be, it's going to be. Ju and I can walk into any park or gym and get genuine love! It is not by accident, but real recognizes real. We have been though the fire and made it out unscathed. We respect the game and the people who respect us. Once people realize what they want from the game, the easier the struggle becomes. We never take for granted Ju's abilities, he just works hard and earns all that come to him. He has been taught to keep a smile on his face and play hard at all costs. There have been ups and there have been downs, but people don't see the hard work, they just see the benefits as a result of it. Also, I am a firm believer in destiny. I played, my wisdom (wifey, keep up) and my pops played. So, it was only right that young Ju and Trey were destined to play too. Like I said they were not forced, wink, wink, into the family business, they just kind of bounced into it and have fully embraced it.

TREY JULIAN, AKA 2.0

It all started as his brother's games. I would roll the ball to the end of the court and Trey Julian would run and get it. He was like the halftime or timeout entertainment. We all loved it, and he would just be all smiles. We never forced him to play hoops, just wanted him to fall in love with it organically. Never trained him or did workout drills, but he was always around—either at Juju's games, practices, tournaments, or just me working him out.
There was one time when Ju was playing in the Amsterdam Houses and the team didn't have enough players. Our coach asked if we would let Trey hoop. Mind you, he was only four and had tennis shoes and cargo shorts on. We said, "What the hell. Sure." And he played pretty good for a kid who had never played any game before. Young Trey was just out there in the 2-3 zone harassing the offense. So, after that night, lightning struck and we were starting all over again, from scratch! From the onset, young Trey was a natural. He didn't have that killer instinct, he just played to play, but it came to him so naturally and effortlessly. He had to have elite sox, pulled up to his knees, the headband and long sleeve shirt under his uniform. He never traveled, just played locally. IS8, Island Garden, and tournaments here and there.

We still weren't convinced if he wanted to really play at the level of commitment to a program or just play for fun. But as time went on, the bug finally bit, and he was in. #theFAMILYbusiness! He began playing with a team from Medina (Brooklyn) that his older brother played for, and the program was family to us. He was playing his grade level and was progressing well. One weekend, he played at Juju's college, and when I say he cooked, HE COOKED! How do you want it, long ball, short ball, drives to the baja (hoop), etc. Trey Julian had arrived in a big way!

Now that Trey was hooping, it was time to look at high schools. We found a school that would fit academics and athletics equally. Although Ju had transferred schools in tenth grade, we did not want to do that to Trey. We thought he would ride with one school for four years, but his coach had a different agenda. Without going into full disgruntled parent mode, let's just say we had to move Trey in the tenth grade because, clearly, he was not in the future plans of the program.

This is always the tricky part of the game. You have some coaches that also have hidden agendas and can kill the spirit of the kids. I say that because Trey's love for the game was diminishing and he did not want to hoop anymore. It was so bad he did not even play on the summer circuit which would have put him in front of coaches and most likely sparked some college interest. So, we, as a family, made the decision to switch schools and immediately he started getting the love that he deserved. It was refreshing to see the smile returning to him while he was playing.

AAU vs. NON-AAU

Growing up, I played travel ball, Catholic leagues and P.A.L. and my Wisdom traveled between the Boros hooping, but it was nothing compared to what we experienced with Ju and Trey. Getting on planes, long bus rides, and long car trips to out-of-state destinations was our life for ten summers straight (Jigga voice) and we loved it!

Playing with the "Program", we were caught up with the hype of "if you stay the course" our kids would earn a free ride to college. On one hand, I wouldn't trade the experience for anything, because not only did we enjoy watching our kids hoop in different venues around the country, but also forming great relationships with parents we traveled with and other parents on the same grind as us. Also, some of the trips doubled as a family vacation due to the events being held during the summer and in vacation hot beds such as Virginia and Florida. With being on the road you see the good and the bad of youth sports. Adults, hangers on, and people who just should not be around kids due to ill will and bad intentions.

The advantages outweigh the disadvantages depending on what you are trying to accomplish. In some sense, if you are aiming for a free education through sports, you need to be in front of college coaches or recruiters to basically audition on a night in and night out basis. This is extremely stressful because as a parent, you are putting a great amount of pressure on your child to perform on a high level. This can cause resentment, anxiety, and overall risk your relationship with your child. On so many levels, you as a parent, really need to come to grips with what is at stake and what is worth risking sanity and happiness.

Life on the road, playing in front of large crowds, and a lot of hostility at such a young age, prepared Ju and Trey to be able to play at high levels later on in their careers. The biggest challenge is letting kids be KIDS! Road trips are essentially business trips, and trying to find the happy medium is always the ongoing theme. It's a catch 22 in the sense that, they are kids, but if you are looking one, two, and three steps ahead, (as I always seem to do), sports is a business and the sooner you learn that the better and less stressful the journey can be. Kids want to be kids, but we as adults and parents need to know and learn how to balance the two worlds of work and play for them, or at least help them through it.

RECLASSIFICATION:
Why do kids reclass? What is reclassing?

Reclassing a child is repeating a grade in school, and it is not a new fad. It is just becoming widespread on so many levels. Is it right or is it wrong? It depends on who you ask and who is doing the asking. Arguments, debates, and extreme disagreements may arise when the subject is brought up. To many on the outside looking in, it is easy to think that families are just trying to get an unfair advantage because with another year, your child may be bigger and stronger than the next class on deck. However, in a lot of cases the child may not be ready emotionally or physically for the next level. The thing about reclassing is, families tend to exaggerate the rules by either trying to use age exceptions in AAU, or in some cases, double reclass saying that their kids have a "late" birthday. In some extreme cases, I have seen some people reclass their kids, then move to a mediocre region and reclass again just so their child can be number one.

In our case, Ju was a year ahead in school and was always in a situation where he could either play his age group, or his grade. It was never really an issue until fifth or sixth grade, when we had to get a waiver to play down. It was then that I started to realize it was becoming an issue. Many people were in my ear about reclassing, but still, me being green and sort of naïve, I never saw the benefits. Back in the day, repeating a grade meant that you were not ready for the next year of school due to academics. You really did not want that on your back. But the funny thing is, now in a lot of cases, it is a badge of honor. Kids don't care about school because they are looking to do the grade over again anyway. Backwards hustling in a sense.

Just because you pull the trigger and reclass, does not necessarily mean that your child will grow academically or athletically (churrrrrrrch!)

After moving to New Jerusalem from New York, Ju had two false starts with two prominent programs. One program wanted him to play his age and not his grade. I had to talk to two of my trusted friends, and I decided that Ju had to play his grade with a Mom-and-Pop type of program. The reason was, at this point, we had no intention of reclassing him. With that being said, we took a break from the major circuit for two years, until he was in the tenth grade. Dealing with high school *politricks* and trying to get a fair shake, we decided to pull the plug and get Ju into a prep (boarding) school and reclass tenth grade. In our case, it was not a sense of trying to get over and play the system. He was just being placed back in the correct grade and in the long run it was to help him mature academically and athletically. All in all, it is about your situation. You cannot run from competition and hide behind reclassing, because at the end of the day it all catches up to you. You also cannot run from the book side of things. At some point you need to buckle down and do your schoolwork and not use the reclass lane as a crutch or an automatic do over. This seems to be a major black eye with this discussion. Parents, 'handlers' and hangers on, depend on the ability to reclass and not care about the academics.

MY NAME IS MY NAME

The city knows the game and now they know the name! The summer of 2012 was one for the books for Ju! MVP of Spring League, several Summer Leagues. We were so proud of him; it's like everywhere he went, a movie was being made. Simply put, he balled out! He became the hired gun, a title that he has never claimed, but since we had no ties to any one team, it was fitting. I am not sure if coaches wanted to reach out in the past and just didn't, but the phone was ringing now. We would get a call, and pretty much, the bat signal would go up, but instead it was the number '3' being displayed in the air. The months of June and July, we were rarely in Jersey. Either I would run home to scoop him up during the week, or we would be out of the house in the city the whole weekend. Mind you, we only had one car, and Trey (aka 2.0) and my Wisdom are not gym or game rats. It would be nothing for me and Ju to break out and hit like three or four parks, chasing the game!

I never intended it to be like this, but the young God was on flames right then, and what did I do? Back off and hit the brakes? Right—I fed the beast, and the kid made his mark! Here is a prime example of a day: we headed to the city, Brooklyn (BK) to be exact, for a morning game. It was Dean Street, first game of the season. We played a team from Newark and Ju played well. His usual coach did not coach, but that was pretty much the soundtrack of the summer. We won and headed to Harlem for a game in City Wide. But me being me, we headed to LES first, because Nike (U Already Know) is doing a workout on this state-of-the-art hardwood court. You feel me, I did say NIKE and one of my friends was doing the workout. I was with one of my guys from BK (he gave Ju his first shot in BK). We stopped and stayed about 30 minutes. Mind you, we still had to get uptown and play. We broke out and got stuck in traffic on the FDR. But, as we always did, we made it! We got into the sweat box of Minnisink, and the game had started. My guy didn't really want to stay, so he gave his son's jersey to Ju.

Show time was on deck! I began coaching, because the parent who was, didn't really want to. I assessed the talent and put Ju in. Parents were looking at me like *really*, and I was like, *you don't know? Sit back and enjoy the show*!

I must say we were kind of feeling ourselves. Because, it had been that type of summer so far. Mind you, we were in Harlem, we had known the director of Citywide for years, but a lot of folks were still sleeping on the young God. We were playing kids we just finished seeing in BK—that's how it was, one park to the next. Same kids, different circumstances).

We were down, but Ju was like *let's go*. Hit a long ball, hit a floater, and he was starting to simmer. Kids on his team were good role players, and he was not being selfish, it's just that in basketball it's a movement and the time is NOW! We were back in the game, probably down one or two at the half. I was doing my best to keep the kids into the game and happy with playing time, all while I could feel the darts being shot at me by parents sick that Ju was showing out and that I was coaching. But hey, *are y'all here to win, watch the show, or want to complain*?

We were down and Ju got the ball, headed up court on the left. He boogied, shifted, crossed a kid at the top of the key, made the kid fall. The embarrassed kid got up and ran to Ju, fouled him while shooting a trey ball. *Face, splash, hold that*! The gym was definitely in a frenzy, and I was doing my best not to smile, laugh or show any emotion. Even though my inside voice is telling me, "It's over, the hell with the score". Let's leave the gym!

We completed the four-point play and we were down one or two points. We were trading baskets and it came down to the last play. Ju was double teamed and had to pass. Kid dribbled off of his foot. We lost, but Ju definitely put on a show! It got to a point that you couldn't worry about the wins and losses, as long as you played well—and the youngin' had done that!

Juju played with Jersey City Boy's Club at a game for the first time and boy was that an experience. This was a tournament in which the winning team in each division wins new uniforms for each player. He was initially supposed to play with the team and coach from New York that he had played with for the last four years. It didn't work out. But he proceeded to use the tournament as his reintroduction party, pretty much letting people know what he was capable of in case they forgot! After that weekend, there was no forgetting. The reason being, we had moved to New Jersey and hadn't been on the AAU circuit for almost a year. Even though Juju had been on the scene for years, it was like the saying, "Outta sight, outta mind".

The first game was against a team and players that he had faced the last couple of years, New Rens. The game was tough and went down to the wire. Juju had the ball in his hands, as he usually did with the game on the line. He drove hard to the right, baseline drive floater. Hit the rim and bounced to the top of the backboard and fell in. GAME! Next!

And next was his arch nemesis, The Riverside Hawks. He had a lot of history with this team. Juju had lost and beat them on many occasions during his time with the program. But this was the first time that he was facing this caliber of competition with this new team. The game was going back and forth, and Ju was doing his thing. At the end of the second half, he was getting emotional and frustrated and went to the bench and cried. The coaches did not know what was going on because they had never witnessed him do this. But as everyone up and down the East coast knew by now, Juju took every play to heart, and it only made him play harder. Riverside had chances to put the game out of reach, but the foul shots were shaky. They were up one or two and Ju had the ball. Time was winding down, tic, tic, tic, tic. . . he got to the top of the key and let it go! Long ball, trey ball, downtown bomb—it was in the air for what seemed to be an eternity. SWISH! *Let's go!* The kid did it again. Two major programs in the same day—a couple of hours apart.

This type of showing was one to cherish. Not because he's mine, but Young Ju was on fire the whole summer. He had his best game during the HITS All Star weekend. He finished the game with 21 points and 15 assists. He did it on an array of blow byes, crossovers, in/outs, long balls, short balls. He was calling out defenders. It was really a sight to see. Another game lost, but it was not because of lack of effort. And we had to run to BK for a Dean Street game (summertime in the city).

He is back playing for his coach and a player on the team he didn't really vibe with (long story but check chapter 6). We get there and he is kind of sluggish—*hello*, he just put on a show at the beach. He was deferring to this other kid. Well, the kid was not delivering, and Ju's coach was barking up a storm. Light switch must have turned on, because next thing you know the young God proceeded to show out. I scan the crowd hovering on the fence and some people were not too happy. Juju had just stolen the show and once again the crowd was in a frenzy! Whether it was the no look passes, pinpoint dime (assists) or floaters, or killer crossovers. Whew, what a sight to see. The kid had the goods!

LOYALTY and LOVE:
The Underdog

College hoops were over, and statistically it was the best year, team-wise. But nothing could change the narrative of what wasn't supposed to happen: being the underdog, underappreciated on so many levels. I remember a coach from the Program who said, "He can't get out of his own way and is uncoachable". Juju was never uncoachable. He was just taught to speak up for himself, and when he saw or experienced negative or unfair treatment, to fight it. We always stood by him, even though at the time, you as a parent, think what the hell is wrong with my kid, because you are (or at least I am) blinded by the smoke and mirrors that you are fed by a lot of these men who are supposed to have your young King's best interest at heart.

No, you have to be loyal to you and yours only, because these coaches and people in positions to help have hidden agendas, hands out, and ulterior motives. So, when you as a parent are trying to find a program for your child, make sure that you are not just going for the glitz and glamour, all the shiny prizes, and just go with who will teach and grow with your child.

And you have to know what the end goal is, the big picture. At the end of the day, most—not all—programs are like factories and turnstiles, just churning out hoopers and not worrying about their true futures or development of the youths' character. His high school career was now over and was a true accomplishment.

The fact that Trey was counted out and downright overlooked just like his big brother Juju, him playing so well, was heartwarming and made us all proud. The thing is, Trey was never in the grind early. But he picked it up quickly and progressed and exceeded expectations. Even if we were biased, without pride. He always worked hard, was hard on himself, and he never wavered from his confidence in his ability. That must be respected on any level.

At the end of the day, it has to be you and yours against the world. You never want to burn any bridges, but always keep your sanity, composure, honesty, and integrity all the way. It is always easy to get blinded by the promises, the gifts and being told what you want to hear, but never make decisions based on emotions. Always take it all in, take a step back and sit down to get all the information needed to make sound and precise decisions. As a common theme throughout this book, the end game has to be well-thought-out to make sure that your child is happy, enjoying the process, and to get what they want out of the game.

The journey will be long-lasting and fulfilling. Always remember, the ball will stop bouncing one day!
#HAPPINESSISFREE

The End

About The Author: *PLAYER/COACH*

Wisdom: *SMALL FORWARD*

Basketball is what brought Tracy and I together. We met at open gym in college and the rest is history! Since we both loved basketball so much, naturally we were eager to place one in the hands of both of our sons. Thus began the AAU journey.
I couldn't have asked for a better best friend, partner in life and love, and most importantly, in parenthood to guide our boys thru this life of basketball. He is truly a walking basketball encyclopedia. His passion, knowledge, observation, and love for the game will be evident in this book!

Juju: *POINT GUARD*

The man with the plan, true man of his word, a family man and leader of others. His actions will never be forgotten by those around him and his love and passion will live on forever.

Trey Julian: *POINT GUARD*

My father is more than just a father, a dream chaser, a shoulder to lean on and look up to, making sure his whole family is taken care of before helping himself. To see him help his family influences me to help the people around me.

Made in United States
North Haven, CT
28 August 2023

40808116R00020